The 101 Commandments of Networking

(Common Sense But Not Common Practice)

by

Janice Smallwood-McKenzie

ISBN: 1-58500-444-8 (Paperback)

Printed in the United States of America
Bloomington, IN

This book is printed on acid free paper.

1st Books - rev. 06/28/04

To Order More Books

To order additional copies of this book, simply log on to the Internet and go to:

www.AuthorHouse.com

Or, you may visit your local bookstore and ask for *Ingram Print-on-Demand Books* from the *Ingram Books-In-Print Database.*

Acknowledgements

This book would not be possible without the support of my dear husband and biggest cheerleader, Homer "Mac" McKenzie, Mommy and Lee, Daddy and Vernell, Brenda, Robert, Linda, Raymond, Nick, Donna, Gena, Sandra, Tracy, Adrianne, Melvin, Marcia, Reggie, Lori, Paula, Ceola, Gail, Cordie, Obie, Denise, Dierdre, Bart, Elenore, Kim, LaSandra, E. Jean, Hope, Sheila W., Sheila W., Sheila F., Beverly, Pat T., Pat H., Candida, Bishop and Mrs. Charles E. Blake.

I extend a heartfelt thank you to Mrs. Hazel O'Leary, Barbara, Nathan, Keith, Bonita, Judith, Skip, Julia P., Gretchen, Willis, Graycee, Margaret, Ruby, Vennie, Lula, Shellie, Alma-Ruth, Dante, Alease, Ranza, Verna, Naimah, Lena, Joan, Mark, Jackie, Greg, Morgan's Heavenly Home, Lindsey & Associates, FMG Media Group, the Black Business Association, Voices, Inc., and the Lorraine Jackson Foundation.

Also, thank you to Mr. Kuribayashi, Mr. Shiraki, Mr. Takenouchi, Mr. Satoh, and Maki, san. And to one of the nicest ladies I've had the pleasure of knowing and working with, Adriana.

About The Book

"The 101 Commandments of Networking: Common Sense But Not Common Practice" is a unique compilation of tips intended to help improve favorable business and personal interactions. This book provides enlightening advice on the simple practices of networking, kindness, sincerity, and acceptance that will help you to reconsider your current methods of networking.

In a straightforward list format, Ms. Smallwood-McKenzie has outlined several simple concepts to boost all kinds of relationships. With much enthusiasm and honesty she offers a guiding manual for the faltering business person or a participant in society's rituals of church, business meetings, receptions and career.

This is a creative and compassionate work that includes tips on listening, openness, and even humor. "The 101 Commandments of Networking: Common Sense But Not Common Practice" is written in an easy-to understand conversational tone and often shares anecdotes from her own experiences to underscore important topics.

www.101NetworkingCommandments.com

Forward

This common sense approach to dealing with people is a must read for anyone in business or the public eye! Mrs. Smallwood-McKenzie gently guides the reader toward goals of self-improvement with spirited prose and enthusiasm.

101 Commandments of Networking is the "Handbook" on making the best of each personal encounter. From 1 to 101, Mrs. Smallwood-McKenzie provides both ABC's and 1, 2, 3's of making human encounters both positive and productive.

Take risks of kindness and inclusion (#24 & 52), be sincere (#37), be honest and pleasant (#90), are some of the commandments we know, but don't always practice. I am encouraged by this book to learn new commandments and practice the old ones.

If you would learn and apply just two (2) commandments every week, you will become a social giant in just one year (52 weeks). Watch yourself grow!

Lula Ballton, Esq.

A Special Note ...

For the last sixteen years I have enjoyed a wonderful career as an administrator in the field of science and technology. I continue to enjoy an environment that brings me into contact with many faculty and students from around the world.

Oh, what to do with so many different cultures and personalities? Not to mention, I am of a different culture and personality from the faculty and students.

Two words come to mind: Deep Respect. You see it is my belief that if you have "deep respect" for everyone whom you come in contact with, that contact will be positive.

A physician once wrote, "...but in every nation the man that fears him and works righteousness is acceptable to him." Am I better than he that's spoken of in this passage is? No. Therefore, it is my responsibility to treat all men (and women and children) with deep respect. But, what about those who don't believe in God? In my environment I meet such ones.

The greatest man to walk the earth said, "...Continue to love your enemies." Another responsibility is laid upon us all: to love our enemies. It is important to understand that those that do not believe in God are not my enemies.

Therefore, if we are to love our enemies all the more to love those we come in contact with each day of our lives. Every man, woman, and child has a responsibility to have deep respect for one another and to show love to all.

This brings me to this publication, "The 101 Commandments of Networking: Common Sense But Not Common Practice." My lovely sister, Janice, has titled this book with the word "networking", and I believe she has accomplished two things with this publication:

1) She has offered an easy way to learn Networking Skills - No doubt this is the book to enhance your skills with business contacts and in the everyday workplace.

2) In addition, Janice has found an easy way for all to "practice" deep respect and love for others. By the way, commandment number one is LOVE.

Janice, you've done a great job! I've always said that you have a heart that is bigger than outdoors.

With deep love and respect,

Linda

THE 101 COMMANDMENTS OF NETWORKING

www.101NetworkingCommandments.com

Commandment 1

Love

When we choose to simply love, our giving and receiving becomes unconditional. We can listen and not be caught up in the vicious cycle of judgment.

We can also watch people and suspend judgment because we are learning to understand that our perception of an individual's behavior does not make it so. This is the essence of love.

Ms. Armstrong, once said, "I keep the telephone of my mind open to love and peace, when fear, doubt and negative call they get a busy signal, soon they will forget my number."

Commandment 2

Smile

A smile makes us appear approachable. Some people are scared by a smile simply because they are not accustomed to unsolicited warmth and acceptance.

Everyone needs acceptance. If we do not reach out and smile, who will? Smile just for the beauty of smiling. It takes 72 muscles to frown, only 14 muscles to smile. Put your muscles to good use and smile.

A smile, like a butterfly, brings beauty to the world simply through its existence.

You can create the same experience by sharing your smile.

Touch

We are inclined to take the art of networking for granted. In doing so, we inadvertently violate unspoken laws governing communication. Be considerate of personal space. Upon meeting someone new, do not assume it is okay to touch him or her.

Be mindful that communication is 7% words, 38% tone/inflection and 55% non-verbal.

Be careful of your non-verbal messages, especially when you are dealing with the opposite sex. Use caution until you can safely determine that your new contacts, friends and loved ones are comfortable with touching. Once you learn this, you are free to enjoy touching as part of your communication.

Commandment 4

Humor

Although humor is a quality that we all possess, we are usually somewhat reluctant to display it. Humor eases pain, releases burdens and can keep your stress levels down, use it! Learn to literally live until you die.

Oliver Wendell Holmes said, "Most people die with the music still in them, while others live their lives desperately looking for the music."

A friend recently made reference to a delightful person with a pleasant spirit who made his transition. She was very sad by the loss of this person whom she did not know personally. I asked her why was she so sad, she remarked that whenever she saw him, he was so very pleasant and she missed the beauty of his spirit and his humor.

See Commandment 88.

Commandment 5

Laughter

Laughter, like humor, will keep the blues away. Many times we laugh at others, but the true secret to the benefits of laughter is being able to laugh at yourself. Enjoy yourself; you are going to be with yourself for the rest of your life!

Other people want to be around people who enjoy laughing and will go out of their way to include them.

Most of us enjoy being around people that can bring the beauty of laughter to our atmosphere. I still enjoy watching "I Love Lucy," after all these years it still makes me laugh.

Commandment 6

Lagniappe (Lan yapp)

This is a southern term, which means "a little something extra," simply share an extra portion of your kindness, joy, peace and patience with those you meet. It is nice to be important but more important to be nice.

That little something extra will create goodwill, trust and inspire confidence, which will make you an excellent candidate for the job, contract or business venture.

I'll give you that little something extra at the end of the book, so keep reading.

Commandment 7

Warmth/Care

When it comes to networking and warmth, sincerity is the key element. That sincerity guides the spirit of networking and is what sets this book apart from the dozens of others providing networking advice.

The power of genuine concern, particularly when it comes to networking, can be summed in the advice passed down by our grandmothers. "People do not care how much you have and how much you know, until they know how much you care."

Kindness

Just as courtesy is contagious, kindness often begets kindness. Anything good is worth repeating and most people will reciprocate.

Those that consider your kindness suspicious usually find it hard to be kind to others without a hidden agenda. When they reflect on their experience of giving, they judge others by their own standards of giving. Don't be fooled or fall into their trap.

Keep being kind! This advice is timeless and yet bears repeating. You can find it in Galatians 5:22.

Commandment 9

Joy

Joy, delight and happiness are all feelings that come from within. As you release your higher self to connect with others, it is important to remember everyone you meet will not be happy about your jovial disposition and this is okay.

No one has the power to rob you of your joy unless you provide him with that power. Bear in mind the words of Nelson Mandela's 1994 Inaugural Speech, "As we are liberated from our fears, our presence automatically liberates others."

Your joy can make others suspicious and fearful. You may on occasion encounter this fear in different forms while networking.

God Is Light, Let His Light Shine through You

Like joy, the light you project externally is a reflection of your internal peace. Do not allow others the power to dim your light. You always have a choice to be a thermometer that registers the atmosphere or a thermostat that sets the temperature for the entire interaction.

You can light up the environment; do not let the environment dim your light. If you share the natural beauty of your existence, you will make it a joy to be in your own company and a joy for others to be with you. If you wish to make friends you must first show yourself friendly.

Again, people are more inclined to do business with people who are friendly and positive.

Commandment 11

A Tip from the White House

In observing the presidential state dinners held at the White House, I've observed that the president seats 130 people at 13 tables, ten people per table. Each table seats one representative from the White House and usually one representative from the country of the dinner's honored guest.

Most guests are invited with a spouse. However, what the invited guests usually don't know is that they frequently are assigned seats separately from their spouses.

The networking lesson however, is that you should not sit with people you know at a dinner. Sitting with strangers' will position you to get a broader perspective and to make new friends and to also expand your business.

Commandment 12

Name Badges On the
Right Not your Left

It sounds simple but placing your name badge on the right makes introductions just a bit smoother. It is easier to slap a name badge on the left hand side because we are conditioned to place our right hand over our heart on the left.

However, when meeting an individual we extend our right hand for a handshake. If you can imagine this introduction you can also visualize the smoothness that takes place when you follow that handshake up to look for the name badge.   If the name badge is on the left or difficult to read, the individual is less likely to remember your name.

Just remember it's the opposite side of "The Pledge of Allegiance."

A Kind Word

A kind word, just like love, inspires the composer, the poet and the painter. A kind word insulates a child, gives joy to our youth and aids the elderly.

It raises the fallen and comforts the tormented. It also breaks the ice when we find ourselves in an uncomfortable situation.

We all love to get compliments. You can also use the "Grapevine" to forward on kind things you've heard about someone or their business. Kindness will always travel well.

Good news can travel just as fast too if we make a point to deliver it!

Commandment 14

Give Your Undivided Attention to the Person You Are Speaking With

If you fail to give your undivided attention when listening, it sends a clear message that you are not interested in what the other person is saying.

It's incredibly disrespectful to look around for others while talking to someone.   If you are going to take the time to communicate, be attentive.

Why would anyone want to continue talking with you if you project disinterest?

Remember, Remember, Remember a Name

When were you last called by the wrong name? How did it make you feel? One of the highest forms of flattery is recognizing a person by name.

When we use names we communicate our interest in people as individuals, which serves to build more intimate relationships while networking. It functions almost like a smile. Recognition breaks down the distance in communication and makes more honest communication possible.

Referring to people by their name, invokes a personal touch, and in this day of "High Tech and No Touch," a "Personal Touch" can and will put you ahead of your business competitors.

Give Sincere Praise

Concentrate on praising the action or the task that has been performed and not the person. It could be perceived as an insincere compliment to give a general personal compliment such as you were great!

What was I great at and when? Do not hesitate to compliment someone's attire or a specific action. Empathy is critical in networking.

What kind of feeling comes over you when you are praised for a job well done or told just how good you look? You feel wonderful and you remember the sincere praise.

I Can Top That Story

When people are sharing their special and joyous events with us, they are inviting us to rejoice in their happiness. It is not time to show up their story or experience with a better one.

If someone tells you about the beautiful Lexus she received for Christmas, it is not necessary for you to bring up the Mercedes Benz you just got for Christmas last year.

When it comes to networking, this commandment is particularly important.

It is important that we learn to share in the excitement of others by simply listening and being pleased for the happiness that person is experiencing. Never compete and compare; competition breeds' contempt and bitterness, and comparison creates jealousy.

Subscribe to At Least One Magazine, Business Journal or Sunday Newspaper

When we are reluctant to interact with others due to our limited information about a topic, we quickly focus on the bad, degrading and negative within that topic.

As we read, networking becomes easier because we are confident in sharing useful information.

Before attending a networking event, try listening to your local news radio station. This is a great confidence booster at any networking event. You will be secure that you are armed with relevant information.

Remember, you are in a much better position to talk with people at a business event when they approach you than when you approach them. Approach anyway, but tread lightly in this area.

Share Information

As we give out information, others will be open to share information with us.

The circulation of information enlightens and therefore empowers people. Providing information feels good.

Information is powerful when it is shared.

Be a resource to others, it's a wonderful reputation to have.

Should you feel limited as to the kind of information you can share at a networking event, simply send me an e-mail via www.101NetworkingCommandments.com and I'll gladly provide detailed information to you based on your area of interest and location.

Understand First and Then Seek To Be Understood

It is not only difficult; it is almost impossible to properly respond to someone if you are not clear about what is being said to you.

You cannot respond correctly until you understand what an individual is saying.

Have you ever thought ahead of what someone was saying to you, thought about your answer, and you assumed you knew just how to answer? Only to discover that you were so glad you waited to respond because you would have been completely embarrassed by what you almost said.

Aren't you glad you sought first to understand?

I just breathed a sigh of relief for you.

If You Do Not Have Time to Have a Conversation When Someone Calls You, Make It Known Early

Do not allow a caller to involve you in a long conversation when your time is limited. Always ask the person if you can return the call at a more convenient time. Even asking the person to call you back can sometimes sound rude.

Once you have made the caller aware that you will talk to him later, you must follow-up by returning the call. When you are the caller, make it a habit to ask if you are calling at an appropriate time. Do not make assumptions about someone's time.

Commandment 22

Return All Calls

There is no excuse not to return a call. Return your calls, even if it's only to let the caller know that you are busy at the moment but would like to know if they are calling about something that can wait a day or two.

There are 1,440 minutes in a day and 2,880 half minutes in a day, how can we not find time to return a call. I try to call when I think I will catch the answering machine/service on. I leave long messages full of information and I spend a maximum of 2 minutes per call. Try it!

When you return a call to someone's office, call before 9:00 a.m., at noon, and/or just after 5:00 p.m. If they are in during these times, they are busy. Let them know that you are aware they are busy and ask if they would like to call you back at their convenience. At least you returned the call.

Acknowledge By Way Of a Call, Card or Thank You Note All Personal Information, Non-Occasion Cards, News Articles And Any Gifts Received

I certainly hope all of my friends make a note of this. When anyone takes the time to send you anything or perform a good deed for you, it is important that you acknowledge that you have received what was sent and appreciate it. Part of the joy in giving is knowing that the receiver appreciates what you have done. Remember, saying thank you goes a long, long way and it inspires repeated acts of kindness.

Please read Commandment 51 three times.

Consider and Include the Guest Accompanying the Guest

Can you recall having a conversation with an individual while someone else was present and the person was never acknowledged? When that happens it's almost as if they did not exist.

If you approach someone and they have a guest standing or seated with them, always acknowledge the guest.

When appropriate include the guest in the conversation by looking into his or her eyes as well as looking into the eyes of the person with whom you are speaking. This tactic insures that everyone feels included in the conversation.

Follow-Up Meeting Individuals with A Call or Note

If you are not interested in an individual, do not ask for their business card.

Your first follow-up connection is only the beginning of creating rapport.

This is all part of networking and effective networking will net you sure returns.

The more you give, the more will be given unto you. Networking is really a game of giving and receiving.

Commandment 26

Update Your Business Card File

On an average one person can collect about 150 cards a year. What purpose will the cards serve if you are not networking?

How can you network effectively if your communication is minimal? You should stay in contact even if it is for no other reason but to keep your files current. Networking works if you utilize your network!

The power of your Rolodex can be a phenomenal asset to your business.

Keep in mind; it is not whom you know, but who knows you and what you do that can make a difference when it comes to business.

If You Cannot Help An Individual, Tell Them You Cannot

Often we listen to someone detail his or her situation even though we know early on that we are in no position to help.

Do not commit yourself when you know that you are unable to help. Negligence in updating our networking contacts is felt no more acutely then when we are unable to supply information or help someone with a problem. There is nothing wrong with being a good listener but when asked for help be frank about your abilities. Do not mislead contacts.

Commandment 28

If You Do Not Understand, Say You Do Not Understand

It is wonderful to speak with someone and have the opportunity to ask that individual to clarify something you do not understand. It is a compliment to the speaker.

Clarity is crucial in networking. By asking for assistance you are giving the other person an opportunity to share his knowledge with you in a more developed way.

Also, by asking for more information you validate the information being provided which in turn, makes that person feel good and feel important.

28

When Someone Calls You, Be Enthusiastic About Their Call

A dead voice and response often begets a dead voice and response. I find it difficult to share with a non-responsive person, which leads me to ask myself, why did I place this call?

It is important to put a "smile" in your voice when answering the telephone.   Our attitudes are contagious and as the saying goes, "Is yours worth catching?"

Commandment 30

When You Receive a Call, Thank the Caller for Calling

Sometimes a caller does not want anything other than the chance to extend a warm hello and to let us know that we are thought about fondly. It is an extended courtesy and should be acknowledged.

Don't call and tell someone you are just calling because you were thinking of them and then all of a sudden, remember that you need a favor.

People can tell when you are not being upfront with them and it is insulting. Be honest with your callers.

Remember, keeping in touch is a gift.

Leave your Shackles at Home

There are many levels of bondage and most bondage situations manage to keep us from growing.

Growth allows us to see potential in others. When we do not allow ourselves to be open to the experiences of others we confront a major roadblock in realizing our own growth potential.

Another level of bondage is when we judge the experiences of others and start comparing those experiences with our own. Then we want to cast our spin on someone else's experience.

We start to deny the truth in the experiences of others based on our own past experience. Try to remain open to seeing some situations as others see them.

There's a lot of truth in, "One man's pleasure is another's poison!"

Commandment 32

Make It a Joy to Be In Your Own Company

A mirror can be a wonderful tool in self-development. It does more than allow you to watch yourself as you interact with others.

However, only through attempting to see ourselves as others see us can we determine if we are pleasant to be around!

If you have not been invited to join others lately, this would be an excellent time for you to position your attitude for success.

Remember the basics, "people like people like them," and pleasant people always want to be around other pleasant people. It's great positive reinforcement.

Accept the Fact, You Will Be A Big Fish in A Little Pond As You Develop Your Networking Skills

Opening up to others is not the norm. Please do not be misguided because everyone you attempt to speak to will not speak back to you, nor will those you smile at, smile back at you. Smile anyway as stated earlier.

The good has a way of coming back to you at the most appropriate times, if you are sincere.

As a great poet once said, "You cannot sprinkle perfume on others without getting a little on yourself."

Commandment 34

Take the Risk of
Introducing Yourself

One very important approach that keeps me encouraged when I am introducing myself to others is: I am looking to share, give, encourage and to be of service to others.

The comfort in that thought is, I can truly say, if I am rejected it is truly their loss since I am not seeking to gain but to give.

However, SUCCESSNET says it best, "Givers Gain."

How many times have you've been glad that you went the extra mile to make a connection with someone that continues to be a positive force in your life today?

What would have happened had you not stretched for that connection? Now imagine the business you've received and the relationships you created for other people not just for yourself due to your willingness to go that extra mile and introduce yourself.

After Introducing Yourself
To Others Ask Them
To Introduce You

Although this too can be risky, introductions by others can be a very powerful networking tool. It's actually a silent endorsement. Be able to ask openly and honestly to meet others.

If there is a reason for needing to make a connection you should share that reason with the person making the introduction. Then the person making the introduction might be able to advise you how to best make the connection.

This can be a humbling experience. Again, remember it is only through serving others that we ourselves can be served.

Find out what their needs are and assist, direct and refer as you make new connections.

Do Not Be Intimidated by "Why!"

Many have learned the power of asking or answering a question with "why?" The tone in how it's asked can be the determining factor as to how best to respond. You should stay alert and pay attention to the tone of questions.

It is an unexpected response and the unexpected can be intimidating. Do not be caught off guard.

One of the wonderful things about being asked "why" is the opportunity to provide an honest answer and more information.

Commandment 37

Talk to People, Not At Them

Talking at people is a behavior easily overlooked and should not be acceptable.

It usually falls-in-line with being over-confident with your *job* title, how much money you make, your degree, where you live, what you drive and basically any attitude that endorses the "Big I, Little You" syndrome.

My suggestion for ridding yourself of this level of consciousness is (1) remember, where you are in life is not always where you end up, and (2) it is nice to be important, but it is still more important to be nice.

Leave the Guilt and Fear at Home or at the Cemetery

Guilt is baggage and fear is bondage. If we are reluctant to grow, or meet and get to know others due to constant reflection on what went wrong five years ago we would never be able to network effectively.

When networking, I recommend that you do not carry baggage from the past. Old baggage will only contribute to mental anguish and feelings of guilt, which will eventually block us from taking the risk of meeting and sharing with other people.

Fear as we know it, is false evidence appearing real. This sets in when we start forecasting the actions or responses of others. Aristotle said, "We learn to play the flute by playing the flute." We also learn effective communication by communicating.

Commandment 39

Remember Words Build Up, Tear Down, Encourage, And Discourage, So Choose Your Words Carefully

When we speak negatively to our friends and love ones our words can have a lasting impact. Many times words that are spoken in jest, anger or meanness can break a person's spirit.

While networking, we need to be aware of the consequences of what we say.

Before speaking we should consider what impact our words will have. Consider whether they will encourage and build up or whether they will tear individuals down. Choose your words wisely. Once words are released, there is no way to get them back and words have a way of following you!

Commandment 40

Ask For What You Really Want

It does not make sense to know what you want and not ask for it. Always remember there are only two answers you can receive "yes or no."

You must also remember that the person you are asking has the right to say no. Never be discouraged if the answer you receive is not the one you are looking for. Be persistent and you will eventually get the answer you want, perhaps from another source.

By the way, the more no's you get, the closer you get to a yes!

Also, be careful of the source; don't take no from a source that is not qualified to give you a no!

However, consider the rule of banking, "No deposits, no withdrawals." You must make deposits into the lives of others!

If You Are Not Feeling Confident, Perhaps You Should Reconsider Attending an Event

Sometimes due to social pressures we find ourselves attending parties, receptions, community events and other gatherings more often than we'd like.

There was a term several years ago about being a wallflower or holding up the wall.

A wallflower is a term that refers to a person who stands in the same place and is not sociable. If you are not feeling good about yourself you are in danger of becoming a wallflower. Your body language will be an obvious sign to others that you are not in the mood to network.

Some say "Fake it until you make it." I disagree with that statement. If you are not feeling good about yourself, reconsider attending an event.

Commandment 42

Back to Basics, Say, "Hello!"

Why wait for someone to speak to you? A sincere hello or congenial greeting such as, "good morning/afternoon" never hurts anyone. No one has ever died from being friendly.

The worst that could happen is that the person might not respond to your greeting. Quite honestly, many individuals do not expect to be greeted so instead of greeting someone first, they act as if they do not see that person.

How *sad!* Remember a person's first impression of you is the basis of any relationship we initiate with them.

Commandment 43

Be Pleasant

Although self-explanatory, it is important to remember that being pleasant includes having a level of balance and an agreeable disposition that does not contradict what your kind words express.

There is a fake corporate smile that people wear to make others think that they care or have a pleasant disposition, and people can see through the phoniness.

Just remember, a sincere smile will always reach the eyes.

Don't let others cause you to be unpleasant to people based on their encounters with them. It's important not to make an enemy of anyone. Think about the person you chose not to like because someone you liked didn't like them, you put them off, and your friend ended up being friends with just that person. It happens!

Let Your Input Be Positive

Again, back to basics of human relations, everyone has been told once "if you do not have anything good to say, try saying nothing."

If you say something negative and it reaches the person, confess, apologize and move on.

The days of being entertained by gossip are over and it is just a matter of time before the tables will turn and not in your favor.

Commandment 45

Etiquette Counts

As business owners, consultants, corporate leaders, and politicians we're hosting meetings over breakfast, lunch, and dinner. Keep in mind effective networking certainly includes proper etiquette.

Master the basics of proper dining. Your drink is on the "right" (5 letters); your bread/food is on the "left" (4 letters). Your fork is on the left, start from the outside in when you have more than one fork. Your spoon and knife are on the right. Don't butter your bread all at once, but butter it piece by piece as you are eating it, and please do not use your napkin as a bib... your napkin should be placed on your lap!

Don't talk with food in your mouth. Don't start eating before the host starts to eat. Trust me, this all matters.

You cannot go wrong picking up an etiquette book (refresher) by Emily Post. You'll be glad you did! You wouldn't want to take a potential client's or your bosses' fork or bread by mistake would you?

Commandment 46

Image Counts Even on Friday

What have we done by implementing Casual Friday?

The last thing we should do is to dress down because it is Friday! We should always want to dress up and not down.

How many times have you gone somewhere and saw someone you wished you had not seen because you were not looking your best? Admit it!

"It is better to not have an opportunity and be prepared than to have an opportunity and not be prepared."

We never want to make excuses for not looking our best and the only way to do that is to always look your best. Wherever you go, you are always representing "You, International."

Small Talk

Networking is not so much meeting, greeting, showing and telling as it is asking. This is where we can really shine.

I am not suggesting that you neglect yourself but that you give others the opportunity to be center stage. Next time you visit someone's office, look around and see what's on their wall. If it's their accomplishments, awards, degrees, children or grandchildren, dog or cat just simply make mention of whatever you see.

Watch that small talk turn into big talk, which turns into big business for you.

Small talk, believe it or not, takes little effort and it is an excellent skill to master.

Acknowledge The
Efforts of Others

How many times have you been invited once to an event, sent one card or given tickets to 1 game?

The power is in having others want to do for you again and again. Sometimes we think, oh, that was kind of nice but that was not what I wanted and we cast the kindness aside.

If you are grateful and appreciative, it is only a matter of time before you will get exactly what you want. In the meantime, keep saying, "Thank you!" graciously and writing those notes!

See Commandment 51.

Commandment 49

Include Individuals in Projects, Parties, Workshops and Events

How many things in life can you do without the help of other people? If you do not include others, you will only be included and invited for a while, if at all.

An Italian poet once said, "Each of us are Angels with only one wing and we can only fly embracing each other."

I can't say it enough, "Networking is about giving, giving, giving and receiving."

Beware, sometimes when you always do the inviting, people think you're so connected and they might not include you.

Simply share that you'd like to be invited and included as well.

Commandment 50

Ask Open and Sincere Questions

Others will sense your interest. Do not become a question asker, if there is such a person. Be direct when asking what you really want to know.

You do not have to keep asking questions over and over just to keep the conversation going. It is okay to be silent.

Be careful not to invade the privacy of others.

Commandment 51

E-Mails Are Not Proper
Thank You Notes

It is my guess that you can think of at least 12 different people that have given you a gift in the last year.

The trouble is there was no repeated giving. Perhaps, you got an invitation and never were invited by the same company/individual again.

Ask yourself did you take the time to acknowledge the kindness with a proper thank you note?

In this day of "High Tech," many are sending thank you notes via e-mail, which is not an acceptable thank you note. E-mail never takes the place of or stands out as much as a handwritten thank you note.

Introduce Individuals
to Each Other

Great people know how to introduce others. I never knew how important this trait was until the "First Lady" of my church introduced me to everyone in her presence. Not only was she gracious in her introductions, but also she never betrayed any difference in status, gender, income or education when giving the introductions.

In her presence you will always be introduced to anyone who has stopped to speak with her, child or adult. This practice is automatic with her and I am proud to say, I have incorporated this technique into my networking lifestyle.

This is also a wonderful way to escape from a conversation.

Commandment 53

If You Cannot Remember a Name for an Introduction, Create a Way for the Individuals to Introduce Themselves

Simply ask the parties present to introduce themselves. I always say "hey guys (girls included) you should know each other." I have not failed at this yet.

Keep in mind it becomes easier every time and it helps to maintain a level of enthusiasm as you do this. Only you will know whose name you forgot.

Also, if you ask if they've met and pause, they will speak up.

I must warn you, this one requires a little practice and a moment of silence, just let that moment past, and they will introduce themselves.

Create a 30 Second Commercial on Yourself and Your Business

This simply involves telling who, what, when, why and how. We put ourselves in an awkward position when we are not prepared. Remember the five (5) P's:

- ❖ Prior
- ❖ Preparation
- ❖ Prevents
- ❖ Poor
- ❖ Performance

Although the power of networking is in listening to others, if someone wants to hear about you, be prepared.

Don't forget to mention a benefit in doing business with you, or be sure to share a success story!

Commandment 55

Don't Just Hand Your Cards Out

When providing your business card make sure your card faces the receiver, it is a nice presentation.

Again, only give your business card to someone from whom you would like to hear. You do not need to provide a card to anyone who asks.

If you think you don't want to be in touch with someone, ask for his or her card instead. Don't put yourself in the position where you must connect with someone you don't enjoy.

Think of obtaining quality contacts, not quantity, you don't have to give your card to everyone.

Commandment 56

Invitations and Donations

In the land of opportunity, everyone is raising money in the name of a worthy cause.

In an attempt to keep up with the network you are building, it can become costly to stay connected.

It is impossible to attend every event to which you are invited once you've mastered networking. Carve out your networking budget carefully so that you will not feel overwhelmed in attempting to attend and support too many affairs at once.

Invitations start to come in at fifty dollars, and suddenly the cost of attending everything to which you are invited is up to $500, $1,000 or more. It's not smart to keep this up if you cannot financially afford to do so. Narrow down your invitations to causes you genuinely care about and send a donation or attend if you can afford it.

Network Or Eat!

Food does not help you network. Eat before anyone arrives and check your teeth for food particles. If you need to think twice about your appearance, you are not going to be confident. You can always eat after the event too.

If you are networking during a meal and need to extend a greasy hand with barbeque sauce, you will remember the embarrassment forever. Strive to avoid potential situations like this one in your networking.

If You Are Networking Effectively, You Will Have Your Goals Prioritized

The days of event marathons are over. Your time is money. Know why you are going to a function and how you plan to service or connect with the people you meet there.

Also, you need to know what you are looking to gain from networking at the event. When we say no to an unnecessary event, we are saying yes to the possibility of being more productive on our own behalf. Say yes to being discriminating when it comes to your time. After all, that is all you have.

As mentioned, discriminating when it comes to events can save you a lot of money.

However, there is no gift greater than the gift of time. Treasure it!

Do Not Allow Others to Make You A Comfort Zone

When you go to an event without a networking agenda you usually end up with another individual who does not have an agenda. If you allow people to exploit your time by pairing up with you, you can miss the opportunity to meet and introduce others.

There is a difference between networking and socializing. We do not need a social agenda to go out and enjoy the company of others or to allow others to enjoy our company.

However when out networking, take note of people who want to spend a lot of time with only you. You must circulate to avoid becoming a comfort zone.

Touch 10-100 Individuals And Let Them Touch 10-100, You Need Not Touch 100-1000 Individuals Directly

Sounds simple, but how many people do you know with an impressive Rolodex who cannot access information for others. Some people we encourage, some encourage us, and some enjoy receiving while others enjoy giving. The art of networking is not about knowing everything and everyone but about knowing a few individuals that know people who know people who know things.

Do Not Adopt the Bad Habits of Others

I am glad to share the correct things to do when it comes to networking because some of us really do not know better.

There are times when people may have no interest in doing the right thing or doing what is politically or socially correct. If someone else chooses to pick their teeth, lick their fingers, put on lipstick, or powder their nose at the dinner table in front of guest, let them do it, you know better.

Networking is a lifestyle, live it!

Do not adopt the bad habits of others.

Shake Hands Firmly
and Remember Rings
Hurt Both Genders

I do not know who came up with the concept of the firm handshake but they clearly forgot about rings.

I have met many people and have shaken many hands and more often than not the women in particular have squeezed my fingers so hard, I just wanted to scream.

While networking we want to appear confident, make eye contact and keep a firm grip for the handshake. Keep in mind though, that both men and women wear rings and a good grip certainly does not need to be painful.

Commandment 63

When Networking Keep In Mind, What Makes an Idea Great Is: It Is Someone Else's Idea and Not Yours, Do Not Be a Dream Killer

You will be amazed at how many individuals are ready and willing to tear down the ideas and dreams of others.

You should always welcome the ideas and imagination of others because generally people are looking for support and confirmation of an idea.

Once we start to criticize, we have thrown-up mental and emotional blocks for that person. Remember that the mind does not hear truth until the heart is prepared. Be gentle and try to be sympathetic when listening to the ideas and dreams of others.

Everyone Is Important

I watched the wife of a political candidate exit from her beautiful Mercedes, without acknowledging the kindness of the valet.

She spoke to me as she approached but this saddened me because not only was the valet important in his own right, but also she missed the opportunity to reach his vote.

Bad news travels quickly. Be kind, gentle and work on making everyone important.

You'll enjoy Commandment 68, "The Networking Factor!"

Your Word Is Your Bond

This is so basic, simple and powerful that I am tempted not to elaborate, but I will because this concept is essential to the fabric of our character.

As you give your word it becomes your commitment. If you say you will arrive at 3:00 p.m., arrive on time or before.

If someone asks you to do a favor and your heart is in it but you know that you just can't do it, state it in advance. This way there are no mixed signals and you remain true to your word.

Commandment 66

Angry People Cannot Hear You

When was the last time you were angry? Did someone try talking to you but you refused to hear him because you were thinking about what you were going to say or because you were simply just too angry.

You can always agree to disagree or simply ask for a moment to take time out to calm down.

Be sure to use time as your friend. You will be amazed by the burden lifted because you let a little time go by. Do not forget to apologize quickly.

Commandment 67

Unhappy People Cannot Hear You

One would think that there is a large population out there simply not hearing you, there is! We can change this consciousness if we work on being considerate of others and creating a third ear which can be called an empathetic ear.

I repeat, "People don't care how much you know, until they know how much you care."

Commandment 68

The Networking Factor

Everyone is important! This is the critical Networking Factor. Be aware of the disadvantage of labeling people based on titles.

Also be careful about introducing who you are and making a big deal of your title. In this changing economy, how many high level executives have you seen on top until the company folded and they became unemployed?

If what you do is the validation of who you are, what happens when you no longer do it?

Mary Kay Ash of Mary Kay Cosmetics was one of the richest women in the world. At the time of her death, she had consultants in 30 countries. One of the secrets to her success was that she imagined that everyone she met was wearing a sign that read, "Make me feel important," and she did just that!

Do Not Take Rejection Personally

Two thoughts come to mind about rejection while networking.

Firstly, rejection might be a request for more information.

Secondly, be mindful of the "kick the dog" theory (the dog just happens to be next to the chair when the angry man sits on the sofa at the end of the day).

It is difficult to give to others what you do not possess. Unhappy people cannot share happiness with you.

It is not realistic to expect them to do so.

Networking Is an Art, Not a Science, Allow Space for Creativity And Remember When You're In Rome, It Is Okay Not To Do As The Romans Do

We can read 500 tips on networking but again Aristotle said, "We learn to play the flute by playing the flute." I say, "You learn to network by networking." Make networking work for you and for those that come across your path.

Always remember, "Networking is simply giving and receiving" and hopefully you will always give more than you receive.

Networking effectively will always be a lifestyle and not a strategy.

Remember Love Comforts, Consoles, and Heals

It is rather interesting watching people listen and then immediately offer advice. Most of the time, people don't want advice. They just want to be heard and to know that someone cares enough to listen.

It is difficult to talk to hurting people and it is hard to prepare your advice for that situation. If you allow yourself to listen, you will comfort, console and heal without saying a word.

Sometimes it is best not to have any advice. It's okay to admit you don't know what to say. It is said that the loudest sound can sometimes be silence.

Networking can be described as "Listening 101."

Commandment 72

"The Apprentice"

What a lesson! Everyone involved on the NBC Television Show Contest "The Apprentice," was vying for the attention of New York's billionaire, Mr. Donald Trump!

Every contestant worked very hard to get the attention of Mr. Trump, on the other hand; Mr. Trump was not counting on the direct connection made with each contestant. Mr. Trump was banking on (a true businessman) the connections made by those who worked for him.

The influence of the subordinates was the deciding factor in determining the winner of the contest.

Be conscious of the manager, receptionist, driver, secretary, supervisor, or vice president. Do not discount or make assumptions about the power entrusted to subordinates.

Commandment 73

Timing Is Everything

How many times have you heard, "The early bird gets the worm?" It is true especially when it comes to effective networking.

Have you ever wondered why so many people continue to talk during the program segment of an event? The mistress of ceremonies is asking repeatedly for the audience to please take their seats so that they can get started with the program, and you have thought why is it no one is listening or honoring the request.

It is because they are having such a good time talking with old friends, meeting new ones and it is enjoyable, but the main reason usually is that they showed up late at the event and missed out on the hour that was set aside for the socializing!

Arrive on time if you want to network!

Let Others Have Their Power

This is touchy because most of us want to be important. Although, I mentioned that everyone is important, keep in mind important is just an illusion.

You are only as important as others make you. So handle your power carefully by making others feel as important as you think you are.

After all, the only way to get what you want is to find out what others want and always give it to them. Most times in return people will give you what you want. This is a universal law of sowing and reaping.

Effective Communication Is a Two-Way Street

This is so simple, yet we seem to have trouble putting it into practice.

If you have trouble letting others have an opportunity to speak just remember that everything you are about to say, you already know.

If you have an opportunity to listen to another person you might learn what they know instead. It is a wonderful opportunity to learn something new.

Volunteer, Volunteer, Volunteer

I cannot stress this enough. Volunteering is so important to your well-being and to the well-being of others. Your self-esteem and confidence will grow because you are helping someone who needs it.

Volunteering also gives you an opportunity to share yourself with others and fill a need. You would be surprised at how many individuals volunteered for a position only to end up with a paying position or contract with the organization or company with whom they volunteered.

How does one get involved as a volunteer? Simply pick up the phone and call an institution or organization in which you have an interest. Speak with the person in charge of operations and express your desire to help the organization and your availability. It really is just that simple. There is no reason for us not to volunteer. Volunteering is part of the foundation of networking.

Commandment 77

Know That It Is Not Always What You Say but How You Say It

Empathy is an important key in networking. When we are empathetic, we are identifying and understanding the thoughts and feelings of others.

If we do a little role reversal before speaking, fewer people will be offended by what we say to them. Think back to the time you were offended by what someone said and how you felt at that time. Propose in your heart not to make anyone feel the way you felt then.

What did you not like about what was said to you? If you did not like it, chances are that no one else is going to like you saying the same thing to them.

We are inclined to treat others as we have been treated. If it was not a good feeling for us, most likely it will not be a good feeling for someone else.

Resolve to make empathy a part of your daily interactions.

Treat All Women as Ladies And All Men as Gentlemen

We are setting an example. If people do not hear what we say, they watch what we do. If we will keep in mind that we are all growing, treating others kindly can become second nature to us.

This is just the "Golden Rule." It's timeless and certainly worth remembering.

Know Your Strengths
And Weaknesses

Have you ever gotten into a heated argument because someone did or said something that you thought was totally out of line, only to discover there were some issues you had not resolved which contributed to your reaction.

With this discovery, perhaps you were not dealing with what created the argument but were dealing with past issues. When you know your strengths, you can accept yourself. Guess what? When you know your weaknesses, you can accept who you are also and not let the thoughts and actions of others put you in bondage or control your emotions.

Know that the Mind Will Not Receive Until the Heart is Prepared

As our grandmothers said, "you can talk to some folk until the cows come home, and they just won't get it!" The reason many don't understand is because the mind cannot hear until the heart is prepared. Angry people cannot hear you.

People who feel that you do not respect them cannot hear you. As the saying goes, "people don't care how much you know until they know how much you care." This bears repeating. Also, remember it is more important to be kind than to be right!

Commandment 81

Acknowledge What You Are Hearing With a Nod

Many of us have taken classes on effective communication and the one phrase we remember the most is "make good eye contact." We can work so hard at looking into someone's eyes during a conversation that we forget to respond to them.

Along with good eye contact, a simple comment is easy. Do not engage them in a staring contest. Instead, listen, comment in a valuable way and look at them normally.

What Makes You Special

I must confess, when I'm conducting seminars, I get such a kick out of asking the participants "What makes you special?" The answers are always enlightening. I have heard comments like my smile, personality, kind spirit, wonderful disposition, upbeat personality, ability to communicate, sensitivity, humility and patience.

Please know that nothing happens until you share your "specialness" with others.

Actually, what makes you special is your ability to make others feel special.

What makes you special is the ability to make others better because they were in your presence.

What makes the great, great? They make others great!

Commandment 83

Be Honest but Careful

This is a tricky area. Sometimes we get so caught up with listeners who have mastered the art of asking questions that will keep you talking.

Without thinking, we answer whatever questions we are asked and later look back and wonder how did we divulge so much information? Be open and honest but think before you speak. It is better to be safe than sorry.

Remember Your Self-Talk

When we articulate what we think to others, they can either accept or reject what they hear. When we start saying negative things about ourselves, like hating our hair or saying we look bad, or are stupid, these words register in our subconscious.

There is power in our words. We have to learn to speak lovingly to others and ourselves. Also, when others take the time to compliment you, smile and accept the compliment graciously and thank them.

One of the best books on this subject is, "Your Word is Your Wand" by Florence Shinn.

Commandment 85

Display Warmth

This is the simplest but by far the most powerful networking tip. We all have so many facets to our personality but I believe most importantly, we all have a warm side. It is important for us to share our warmth with others.

As I said, it is simple but few of us are able to share the real warmth that we have inside with others due to the various masks we wear.

Being warm allows others to feel safe in your presence. When people feel safe with you, they will be honest.

Commandment 86

Be Sympathetic

We have ended up in many conversations advising and using our past experiences and set backs to give others what we think is needed for them to get through their situation.

Despite the good intentions in this strategy, the truth is that most people are just searching for a sympathetic ear.

Commandment 87

Do Not Take Yourself
So Seriously

You will find yourself in many awkward situations and you might be tempted to question yourself.

Learning in life is by trial and error and so is networking. You just do it and have fun in the process. Use your mistakes in life and networking as tools to improve yourself.

Branding

Like the term networking, this term has become a bit over-used. The over usage does not diminish the importance of these two concepts to your success in the areas of business, personal relationships and politics.

How many times have you gone into the grocery store saw a great new product that was packaged well and in your price range?

You picked up the item and put it back down because you were not familiar with the brand? It is the same thing when it comes to individuals. You are building a brand as you network and you want people to be comfortable and confident with your label because they can utilize your goods or services and too refer others to you.

We use to call it reputation, now we call it Branding! Protect your "Brand and your Platform."

Commandment 89

What Is Natural For You

What is natural for others is not always natural for you and vice versa. If it works for you use it.

There are so many regional, cultural, social and economical differences that it is sometimes difficult to understand another person's background.

Think about networking with an individual from another state or country and you will find out just how different we are.

When presenting your business card in Japan, it is natural and expected that you greet one another with a bow, hold your business card with two hands with the card facing the recipient. It's natural for Japanese, simply the norm and what is expected. Does that work in the United States?

Be natural and let others be natural too.

Be Easy To Get Along With

Conversation is not a football game and you need not fight to get a touch down or score conversation points. There is no need to be combative in conversation.

Simply try to be easy to get along with. It is less stressful to communicate and get along because in the end it works out good for all concerned.

To have it said at the end of your life that the world is a far better place because you lived will be the highest compliment! That is a legacy worth striving towards.

Accepting Compliments

This is so hard for some people. Let me tell you it is worth being comfortable with being uncomfortable when it comes to accepting compliments.

Accepting compliments is a lot like getting a gift, and you take the wrapping off the gift, and you think this is not the gift that I wanted, and it shows on your face. Think about it, if you discount someone's gift it's insulting?

When someone extends a compliment to you and you reject the compliment you are discounting the gift of the compliment and the giver of the compliment will not feel good.

Just like you would accept a gift because someone was kind enough to give it to you, you should also accept a compliment because someone was kind enough to give it to you!

Do Not Fold Your Arms While Listening

This is a signal that can often be misinterpreted. I personally fold my arms at times because I have a fat stomach and it's a comfortable resting place for my arms (a joke!). We have been taught over the years that this shows a lack of interest.

We cannot assume others know we might be folding our arms to rest them. It is safe however, to leave your arms at your sides or hold one arm down and the other somewhat in an upward position or maybe even clasp them in front of you.

Commandment 93

Lean Forward To Listen

Interestingly enough, I read an article in the Wall Street Journal about a powerful group of entertainers having dinner at a ritzy Restaurant in lovely Beverly Hills.

When making reference to the entertainer in control and holding court, the first thing the writer mentioned was his posture.

He was "leaning forward," which usually puts you very much in control or it gives others the illusion that you are in control. If you are listening, this forward lean gives others the impression that you are in control of the conversation or the meeting and that you are a great listener.

Commandment 94

Listen As Though You Are Going To Be Quizzed

People just want to be heard and only few of us have mastered the skills of being attentive listeners. This technique will prove to be effective and will allow you to excel while networking.

If you practice listening, as though you were going to be quizzed you will be ready if you need to refer to what was said during your conversation. Automatically, you will have favor with the other person because your keen way of listening shows that you care.

People simply want to know that they are making a difference and that someone cares. Be that someone.

Commandment 95

Get the Facts

It is amazing how what we thought we heard can alter our mood, habits and train of thought. Distorted facts can change the mood, habits and train of thought in others.

It is a given, if we are anxious while trying to listen it is difficult to grasp the facts because our thoughts or anxiety have created automatic stumbling blocks. Remember we think much faster than we talk.

Those little facts can make a big difference in networking. Listen for birthdays, anniversaries, children's names, points of interest, and vacations. It helps you to create that personal touch!

Listen For What
People Do Not Say

Have you ever found yourself asking someone a question and he or she seemed short with you and the response was a simple 'yes' or 'no' even though your question required a more in-depth answer?

I have found that instead of answering falsely, some people prefer a quick 'no' or 'yes' as a response to certain questions. In many instances, people provide this type of response to questions they are uncomfortable answering.

The secret is to ask the correct question and to that end it is good to have an investigative mind. I think it is okay to ask questions to get to the unspoken subject. However be careful, this applies only if you really need to know.

Commandment 97

Remember Every Shut
Eye Is Not Sleep

I cannot figure out for the life of me (as my grandmother use to say) why we assume that we can speak in confidence based on closed eyes.

So many of us have said, "It is okay, he/she is sleeping." Then we are embarrassed by what should not have been openly mentioned. (Everyone at the salad bar is not just getting salad either.)

If eyes are closed, do not assume they are sleeping eyes.

Speak to Strangers

I know this goes against what our mother's taught us, and that was simply never to speak to strangers, and that worked when we were twelve years old.

However, did you ever notice your mother made you call all the strangers in the world auntie, and uncle? What mom was really saying was, "Don't talk to people that I've not approved of yet." That's what she really meant, and now you are old enough to implement the approval system for yourself.

Dismiss that old adage of not talking to strangers, and make it your business to meet anyone that is within 3 feet of your personal space.

Now we can speak to strangers, build rapport, make them our friends, and even do business with them.

Everyone is first a stranger, and this is a temporary condition.

Commandment 99

If You Are Speaking Confidently, State It

How many confidential conversations have you had where you hear the information later? You just assumed the person knew it was confidential.

I am from the old school and this situation is new for many. If you absolutely do not want it told, then absolutely do not tell it. When you state it is confidential, the other party might not take confidentiality to heart as you might.

Be discerning, safe and smart in providing information.

Confidentiality is a very rare commodity in today's society. Be worthy of the trust of others, and stay true to your word.

Commandment 100

No Alcohol/Drinking

If you want to be totally in control of yourself and the situation, don't drink alcohol!

When you're at a business meeting, event, party or reception, leave the alcohol alone. Alcohol can alter your present state of mind.

Remember that we never get a second chance to make a good impression. If you had spent days, months or years building a reliable reputation and you end up tipsy at a dinner party, people will remember you slurring your words and being a little out of character or out of control on the dance floor? You don't want to chance that, do you?

On a lighter note, if you are drinking a soft drink, keep it in your left hand, and your right hand will be nice and dry as you extend it to meet an unexpected guest.

Commandment 101

Be Flexible and Confident in Trying these Commandments

Expressed or unexpressed, we are all connected. Sometimes, establishing rapport requires you to go the extra mile.

Nothing in life is absolute; one man's pleasure is another's poison. I suggest you continue to network and enjoy the journey.

This reference guide is about the spirit of networking, which is based on substance of character, universal principles of sowing and reaping. It is not just about methodology and techniques.

Incorporate "The 101 Commandments of Networking: Common Sense But Not Common Practice" into your lifestyle and you will be blessed beyond measure.

You will simply be sharing your God-self with the world. Praise God!

"Lagniappe"
(A Little Something Extra)
Nine Interesting Ways to Meet People

1. Identify the convention center in your area, send a S.A.S.E. with adequate postage and request a one-year calendar of events.

2. Keep involved in your spiritual life. Volunteer at church.

3. Read as much as possible. Read one new book every month.

4. Become your own best friend.

5. Get along with people from different cultures and attend their events.

6. Create a social-concerns group in your community.

7. Join a Junior Chamber of Commerce and become active in networking with others.

8. Volunteer with the Police Department and other organizations that interact with the public.

9. Identify your sincere area of interest and study that area. As you attend various functions in your area of interest, you will meet others with similar interests.

101 Networking Commandments
Workbook & Exercise Module

Day 1 (2, 3, 4, 5...30)

The commandment I used today.

_____

_____

_____

_____

_____

_____

_____

_____

_____

_____

How this relates to the commandment I used
yesterday.

_____

_____

_____

_____

_____

_____

_____

_____

_____

_____

_____

The commandment I plan to use tomorrow.

_____

_____

_____

_____

_____

_____

_____

_____

_____

_____

_____

Conclusion

In conclusion, I am delighted to share with you that in every journey, you must be present to maximize the experience of the journey to it's fullest.

Just think if you underline the letters, "*u r n*" in the word *journey,* you'll discover it reads *you are in.* As you look further you'll discover the letters "*j o*" to your left, and the letter "*y*" to your right.

When I break this down, it simply reads, "You are in the center of your joy when you are on the right journey." I repeat, enjoy the journey of networking!

I'd love to think that I have given you something deep, new and undiscovered. Not the case! However, this networking guide provides an easy step-by-step approach to networking that works.

Please indulge me as I deliver a proven fact about *acknowledge* spells "edge." Webster reveals that an edge is a superior advantage. Look closer at this word. Let's interpret *"ac"* (act) *"know," "now,"* and *edge.*

Should you decide to acknowledge, or *act* on what you *know* now, you'll have and edge and an *edge* is a superior advantage.

About The Author
Janice Smallwood-McKenzie

www.101NetworkingCommandments.com

Janice Smallwood-McKenzie is a vibrant, intelligent professional who lives what she believes: we need each other. Her perpetually joyous and gracious persona, coupled with her belief, forms the basis for her exceptional abilities in the area of Networking. Whether she is talking or writing about Networking, or coaching her clients, Ms. Smallwood-McKenzie exudes the benefits of individuals effectively connecting with each other. She became an expert in effectively connecting with people through many years of first-hand experience.

Ms. Smallwood McKenzie is a Networking Coach. Under her tutelage, some of her clients have been publicly acknowledged by Hillary Clinton, Maya Angelou, Oprah Winfrey and other notable people across the country. Ms. Smallwood-McKenzie cultivated relationships and contacts with some of the most influential people in the country. Her organizational skills, initiative and willingness to share information and contacts caused her to become depended upon by many as a Networking Coach to assist professionals, solo-preneurs, and small businesses in expanding their personal, business and political bases.

Ms. Smallwood-McKenzie is respected as a woman who is serious about helping people. She is a trusted and valued resource to friends and clients for her skills, wisdom and ability to motivate. "… Her unique style is that of a warm and wonderful angel who knows how to take care of business and inspire everyone else to do the same," says syndicated radio show host Candida Mobley-Wright of Voices, Inc. "She's a Blessing."

www.101NetworkingCommandments.com